Applied Psychology

Volume 12

SPECIFIC

APPLICATIONS

Being the Twelfth of a Series of Twelve Volumes on the Applications of Psychology to the Problems of Personal and Business Efficiency

BY

WARREN HILTON, A.B., L.L.B.

FOUNDER OF THE SOCIETY OF APPLIED PSYCHOLOGY

ISSUED UNDER THE AUSPICES OF
THE LITERARY DIGEST
FOR
NEW YORK AND LONDON
1919

Republished from the public domain by

Creative English Publishing

www.Creative-English-Institute.com

Under Classic Reads

May 2014

ISBN-13:
978-1499593716

ISBN-10:
1499593716

CONTENTS

Chapter III. PAGE 25
SCIENTIFIC METHODS FOR FORTUNE-BUILDING

BASIC PRINCIPLES OF MONEY-MAKING

Chapter I

BASIC PRINCIPLES OF MONEY-MAKING

SUCCESS AND THE AVERAGE MAN

THE vast majority of men success means but one thing — Riches.

In this book we shall show you how the principles and methods set forth in this Course may be applied to the accumulation of wealth. And when we say "wealth" we mean wealth in a literal sense, as signifying the material things you want to have.

PSYCHOLOGY APPLIED TO WEALTH ACCUMULATION

We make but one demand of you, and that is a previous careful study and assimilation of the books that have gone before.

Let us sum up the substance of our teachings to this point with special reference to the acquisition of material things:

1. You must first intelligently formulate in your own mind the one thing you most desire.

2. You must form a distinct and definite mental picture of the thing you want, a picture expressive of purpose, faith and thankfulness in its prophecy of actualization.

3. You must persistently practice Self-Analysis, Study for Knowledge, Mental Demand, Visualization and Affirmation.

4. By these concentrative methods you will summon, control and direct all your mental energies upon the one desire.

5. By these concentrative methods all your outward activities will be un-consciously focused upon the creation of the one object of desire.

6. By these concentrative methods you will develop Psychic Power and Initiative, you will saturate your consciousness with a purposive faith in your success, and unexpected resources of energy will well forth from the sub-conscious reservoir to compass the thing you want.

If you have thoroughly mastered the Course to this point, you will have accepted these statements of basic principles. You will know their absolute truth. You will have the unquestioning faith of one whose mind and reason have been convinced.

MATHEMATICAL CERTAINTY OF GETTING RICH

And you will at once joyously and confidently act upon our teachings, and in so doing you will yourself exemplify their truth.

For the principles we expound are thoroughly scientific. They are as reliable as the laws of physics or geometry.

And it is a mathematical certainty that success will come to every man that follows our directions confidently, intelligently and persistently.

A FINE OPENING FOR THE RIGHT MAN

Chapter II

A FINE OPENING FOR THE RIGHT MAN

CRAFT, CHICANERY AND DOUBLE-DEALING

TO BEGIN with, you must get it out of your head that for you to have more wealth implies that someone else must have less.

The wealth you want and the wealth you must have is wealth you are going to create. It is not necessary to despoil your neighbor. It is not necessary to lie or cheat or steal.

The money that you want does not represent existing wealth. There is no satisfaction in the gain that is another's loss. Besides, it is the most difficult to acquire.

UNAPPROPRIATED MILLIONS

The supply of wealth is unlimited. It is as boundless as matter. For wealth is inert matter molded into useful forms.

Lay aside all thought of craft, chicanery and double-dealing. Put your thoughts to work upon the boundless universe of wealth yet unappropriated.

Untold millions of treasure are yet buried in every square mile of the earth's surface. Part of this is yours. And it will come to you if you do as we say.

Civilization's most profitable work is that of the pioneer. Seven thousand dollars was spent on the voyage of Columbus — and the returns are growing with the years.

PROFITS OF BUSINESS PIONEERING

Ten thousand ships would have accompanied Columbus westward, and their crews would have braved every hardship and peril — if only they had known beforehand what the fruits of the venture were to be. The difference lay in this, that Columbus was willing to stake all on the strength of his convictions.

Every decade sees the discovery of some kind of new world. Printing, steam, electricity, telegraphy, wireless telegraphy, the phonograph, the aero plane — each has revealed a new world; each is but a prophecy of greater discoveries yet to come.

Who will make these new discoveries? What is to be your part in unlocking the wonders of tomorrow?

BASIS FOR UNDERTAKING
BIG ENTERPRISES

Every new world of achievement lies beyond the sea. The biggest things in business are undertaken on faith. Oceans unknown are crossed in following the lead of convictions.

Even now forces may be at work in distant lands upon the building of your fortune.

But you must lay aside all thought of the riches that you see about you. You must cease to covet the riches of other men.

Your fortune may yet be uncreated. It is yours to create.

This does not mean that you are to have no business dealings with other men.

SELLING THAT WHICH IS VALUELESS

It does mean that your business dealings are to be to the advantage of others as well as of yourself. It means that you cannot afford to sell to another that which will be valueless to him.

It means that your fortune is to come out of the creation and distribution of new forms of tangible riches for which all the world will be your debtor.

The oil and canvas and colors that went into the composition of a Rembrandt were in themselves of no value, yet the masterpiece is priceless. The pen and ink and paper employed in outlining a more efficient system for a factory are worthless, yet the outline itself may turn a loss into a handsome profit.

If you are a merchant or manufacturer, your first concern should be to discover just what the people want, instead of pursuing the unfortunate policy of many business men who lay all the emphasis on the making and selling end. It matters not how well made or how artfully offered your wares may be, if they do not meet a real demand you must change your methods or you will fail.

MANUFACTURING FOR EXPORT

Do you know why the United States buys from the people of South America twice as much as it sells them? It is because the manufacturers of the United States do not study the special requirements of the people of South America, but simply try to sell them the same kinds of merchandise that "take" in the home market. Meanwhile European manufacturers get the bulk of South American business by exporting articles specially adapted to South American requirements.

NEW FIELDS FOR COMMERCIAL EXPLOITATION

Success attends the merchant or manufacturer who begins at the beginning with a sympathetic and appreciative mental realization of the needs of others.

The field of commercial exploit is unlimited. Every department of art, commerce and manufacture holds within itself at this moment the germs of countless opportunities for the discovery and exploitation of improvements. Humanity has not reached its zenith with our generation. Human progress will not halt. Each step will be taken as soon as men clearly see it, and the man who is to win is the man whose perceptions are alert and unclouded.

10-CENT STORES AND
MAIL-ORDER HOUSES

The tallest business block in New York City was built by the man who developed the "5- and 10-cent counters" into "5- and 10-cent stores." He was merely doing an old thing in a new way. He was capitalizing an idea.

The mail-order house that goes past the country merchant into the home of the consumer is a great oak that has grown from the tiny acorn of one man's big idea.

All the creative ideas have not been thought. Many a big idea is waiting to be claimed. And the world will award its richest prizes to the claimants.

This is a creative age. It calls for work that is born of creative thought. It calls for work like that of the artist who, when asked what he mixed his colors with, replied, "With brains, sir."

SOURCES OF WEALTH

Matter is powerless, passive, inert.

Mind is Force, Energy and Power.

Mind is King. Mind shapes and controls matter. Matter in useful forms is but the manifestation of consciousness.

The secrets of creation are locked up in the thinking consciousness.

There is no thing but is the embodiment of pre-existing thought. The house you live in was first erected in the consciousness of him who planned it. The aero plane, the steam-engine, the diamond, the dollar — all are but materializations of human thought out of formless matter.

AS TO GETTING RICH QUICK

And back of formless matter was God's Creative Thought.

Every conceivable force and fact arose from MIND in action. And the action of mind is orderly and dependable.

So thus creation presupposes thought. And thought, held in consciousness, tends to create its material embodiment.

How? If you think of an automobile, will it take shape before your eyes? If you think of a cut-glass vase, will it rise up shimmering before you?

By no means. Not outside fairyland does the mind work its way with the magic suddenness of Aladdin's lamp.

The Creative Thought that planned the universe wrought its evolution out of chaos during countless ages.

HOW RICHES ARE REALIZED

The Creative Thought that imaged man in his world is yet working its fulfilment.

The Creative Thought that brings the grain to its day of ripening follows established lines of growth.

The Creative Thought that visioned the Panama Canal found fulfilment through long years and the employment of vast forces.

Creative Thought works no magic transformations. It obeys natural laws. It releases natural energies. It sets in motion natural forces. It attains fulfilment through its conscious and unconscious influences upon you, upon your outward conduct, upon your friends and acquaintances, and upon the whole of your environment.

LAWS OF ACTUALIZATION

You can originate thoughts. You are a thinking unit.

And since thoughts are creative of the things they dwell upon, you can create for yourself the things you think about.

Mark, then, these

LAWS OF ACTUALIZATION

1. Consciousness tends to product the realization of its images.

2. You can control the content of your consciousness by controlling your attention.

3. By controlling your attention you can produce in consciousness the image of the thing you want.

4. By concentrated thinking you can bring all your bodily activities to bear upon the creation of the thing you think about.

5. You can thus cause the creation for yourself of the thing you want.

VIGILANCE, MASTERY, AND POWER IN FINANCE

Every man can do this. Few make the effort.

And no puny effort will suffice. A multitude of influences are arrayed against you. To steadfastly keep your consciousness filled with thoughts of riches, health and life in the midst of evidences of poverty, disease and death takes constant effort. It requires ceaseless vigilance, mastery and power.

But the man who can do this thing can smile in the face of 'Death, can commune with the Mighty, The world lies at his feet.

Specific Applications

SCIENTIFIC METHODS FOR FORTUNE-BUILDING

Chapter III

SCIENTIFIC METHODS FOR FORTUNE-BUILDING

CONSCIOUSNESS OF PERSONAL POWER

IN THIS chapter are given eight regimes for scientific fortune-building, each regime being correspondingly designated by one of the first eight letters of the alphabet.

A. Banish all doubts and fears.

You have the inherent power to think what you want to think.

And, having that power, you can create what you want to create. You can do and be and acquire what you choose to do and be and have.

Fix these principles in your mind.

THE DEFINITE BUSINESS GOAL

Let no contrary ideas intrude upon your consciousness.

Listen to no arguments that would tend to unsettle your faith.

Do nothing, say nothing, hear nothing, read nothing, think nothing that is not in harmony with these ideas.

For these ideas are Truth, absolute and immutable, and it follows that all else is Falsehood or Error.

And having accomplished this much you will have taken your first deliberate and scientific step towards riches.

B. Next determine in your own mind the one definite thing that you want first.

You cannot create anything until you first make up your mind as to just what it is to be.

THE MAGNETISM OF COVETOUSNESS

A mere general wish for wealth will never do. Every man, with one motive or another, has that general desire.

Nor will it do for you to have a mere indefinite longing for the things that money will buy. The child that asks his father for a gift does not couch his request in general terms. He wants one thing, and he asks for it and begs for it and longs for it, and, as a rule, he gets it.

So when you call upon your own segment of the Infinite Mind, the Father of all Good, be sure that you know what you want — what one thing most and first of all.

C. Having settled upon the thing you want, get it clearly in your mind.

HOW TO UTILIZE EVERY OPPORTUNITY

Visualize it. Form a definite and life-like mental picture of it.

The only way to obtain what you want deliberately and scientifically is to concentrate your mind upon it. You must keep its image before your mind as the batsman keeps his eye upon the ball. Let not your attention waver.

The more you hold the picture before your mental vision the more keenly will you covet it. And the more you covet it the more persistently will consciousness cling to its vision.

HOW TO CRYSTALIZE ONE'S AIM

And so will realization come about. For every man you meet, every word you hear, every statement you read, every thing you see, every thought you have, every past, present and future experience of your life, will be tried in the same light, will be put to the same test — the test of adaptability and utility for the attainment of the thing desired. Those that fit into your mental picture will be retained and utilized and will form the springs of action. Those that do not meet this test will be shunted aside into subconscious obscurity.

This selective, process will not be a conscious one. You will know nothing of it. Your thought must be and will be engrossed in your vision.

For know that the more clear and definite you make that vision the more certainly will it be realized.

D. Nor.is this all. Your vision must be conceived in unwavering Faith.

GOING AFTER A GENERAL AGENCY

Therefore, picture to yourself the thing as here. See it as a present reality. See yourself in the picture with it, having it, using it, enjoying it.

Let us suppose that you desire the distributing agency for some article of manufacture. See yourself closing the contract, renting your offices, organizing your selling forces, planning your advertising campaign, doing the thousand and one things necessary to make a business prosper, and then see yourself reveling in a sheaf of orders and laying aside a satisfactory balance at the end of the year.

DEALING WITH AN EMPLOYER

If it be a better situation, with an increase in salary, see yourself doing all the things necessary to make you the man for the place. See yourself applying for it, hear what you have to say in your own behalf. See your employer protesting, objecting. See him waver and yield. Picture all the details of your efforts in the new position, your new ideas, your ingenious devices, and finally your complete and unqualified success. Enter upon all the details of the desired employment in your imagination, hive it menially, and in due time its mantle will in reality descend upon your shoulders.

This does not mean that you will be only a dreamer. It does not mean that the fruits of the earth will come without toil.

But you need not concern yourself with these details.

FORESIGHT AND THE AUTOMATIC CONSCIOUSNESS

Rest assured that if your vision is clear enough, if you really live in mind the life you want to live in the flesh, if all your thoughts are concentrated upon the one goal, then the energy, the application, the persistence, the ability and the work, all that you have and need to have, will be sure to manifest themselves with no further care on your part.

For every idea is a pent-up reservoir of energy, and every idea must find its release in action, and every thought complex has its emotional element, and every harmonized state of consciousness is energizing, purposive and effective.

And if your mental vision is clear, definite and all-absorbing, every experience that you have, every situation in which you may be placed, will arouse a prompt, appropriate, automatic and advantageous response from your intent and watchful consciousness.

LOADSTONE OF PERSONALITY

So your part is simply to concentrate your thoughts, and, doing this, to know that the transfiguration is at hand.

E. Cultivate a cheerful expression. If doubts arise, if anxious thoughts persist in appearing at the threshold of consciousness, a smile, however forced, will drive them into the depths from which they came.

The more unwavering your faith, the more inflexible your purpose and the more vivid the pictures of your aims, the more speedily will come the realization of your desires, the more quickly will you become rich and successful. For every thought you hold tends to manifest itself in action.

MANIFESTING THOUGHT IN ACTION

You know that if you like a man he also is attracted toward you. On the other hand, if for any reason you conceive a feeling of hostility toward him, he quickly draws away. And this, notwithstanding your every care to conceal your feelings, and even though you are serenely confident that you have not permitted any suggestion of them to appear.

Love begets its love, and the one grown cold, the other perishes.

There is a scientific reason for this. Thoughts manifest themselves in bodily action, and the minds of others are alert to interpret the faintest and most fleeting sign.

Know, then, that the thoughts you hold of the things you yearn for will certainly and surely go forth even though unspoken.

ZONES OF THOUGHT INFLUENCE

Thoughts will tincture your environment.

Thoughts will make and unmake friendships and alliances.

Thoughts will permeate the world about you.

Thoughts will create and constitute an aura that will determine your place as a man among men.

As the zone of your thought influence radiates and widens, it will carry with it the impress of your mental vision. Other minds, constituting other units of creative force, will feel the stirrings of your impellent thought. Other agencies will be invoked and other physical forces set in motion to achieve the accomplishment of your desires.

None can foresee the limits of such an influence. Who knows but that by physical impulses unconsciously given, unconsciously received and unconsciously transmitted men and women in distant lands, knowing nothing of you, may ignorantly even now be working the fulfilment of your desires?

Therefore, let no negative thoughts enter your mind, or if they come thrust them from you. Every negative thought in consciousness tends to repress and neutralize the creative thought of your desire, tends to inhibit its expression, tends to express itself in outward action unfriendly to your purpose.

MENTAL BACILLI OF FAILURE

Fear, doubt and worry are the very antitheses of creative thought. Not only do they inhibit its expression, but they set in motion contrary influences and energies.

Why? What are doubts and fears and worries?

Are they emotions? No. They are thoughts. They are mental pictures of yourself in all the circumstances and surroundings that you would like most to avoid. They are a mental chamber of horrors in which you see yourself in failure, poverty, squalor, disease and misery.

Since worries and fears are thoughts, and as such tend to work their hideous reality, shun them as you would a pestilence. They are the bacilli of mental disease. They are the virus of failure.

Just as you have no friends so loyal, rich and powerful as your own creative thoughts, so you have no enemies so wicked and terrible as your own thoughts of unbelief.

Therefore, watch over your consciousness. Scrutinize your thoughts. They set the course that you are sure to follow.

F. Things you hear and see, your environment — in other words, the sense- perceptions that crowd in upon you — operate through the laws of association to make active in consciousness such thoughts as are associated with them.

It follows that scenes of poverty, sickness and wretchedness will make it more difficult for you to hold the right kind of creative thoughts. Your vision will be subtly influenced and clouded by the darkness of your surroundings.

THE KIND OF MEN TO TIE TO

Therefore, associate yourself as far as possible with people in the circumstances you hope to attain.

You cannot fill the purse of poverty while you yourself are poor, nor soothe the sufferings of sorrow while you yourself are in despair.

Talk with the poor about the better circumstances they are coming into. Talk with the sick as convalescents planning on what they will do when well and strong.

Thereby you confer a double favor. You benefit them as well as yourself.

Do not imagine for a moment that to do these things is to become sordid and contemptible.

FILLING THE PURSE OF POVERTY

This would follow if you were trying to get rich at the expense of others. But you are to get rich through creative effort, through the employment of your talents and energies in ways that will benefit others as well as yourself.

The efficiency expert is of more value to mankind than the rich but idle dispenser of charity. The engineer is a more desirable citizen than the mere philanthropist. We have all admired the extent of Carnegie's liberality and the form of his benefactions, but the acceptance of such princely gifts may tend to cultivate a beggarly spirit in a democratic people. And the value to the world of engineer and efficiency expert lies not only in their material achievements, but also in the uplifting influence of their careers upon the spirits of men.

UPBUILDING A GREAT INDUSTRY

What the poor need is not sympathy.
It is not charity.

It is Inspiration. It is Opportunity.
It is the inspiration that makes its own opportunity.

To get rich through the upbuilding of a great industry, through the laying bare of new sources of wealth, through any form of creative achievement, is the loftiest aspiration you can take into your heart, for it assumes and implies the furtherance of all noble aims.

G. Do not waste your time in wondering if you will succeed or in considering just what step to take first.

BEING A MAN OF ACTION

If your mind is sufficiently possessed with purposive thoughts of what you are to have and what you are to be, everything else will take care of itself, your every action will be colored in the dye of your desire. Your singleness of purpose will enable you to meet satisfactorily every emergency.

No man with thoughts concentrated upon a mental vision can postpone his efforts to attain it. It is in the very nature of mind and body that he should act now.

If he is in the wrong environment, if he is in the wrong kind of work, if he is in the wrong place, these facts will unendurably gall his spirit. He will — nay, he must! — wrench himself free though the heavens fall.

He will put his every ounce of energy into present action.

He will do no waiting for things to turn up. He will work and strive and struggle as if each day was the only day he had to live.

He will fit himself for the place he means to fill. He will fit himself to use wisely the things he means to have. He will fit himself to wear bravely the honors he means to win.

And while thus holding the vision of the future he will realize that his every act here and now will be for him either a step forward or a step backward, a positive success or a positive failure, according as it does or does not bring him nearer to the thing he craves.

H. Practice persistently, devotedly, as the swift and sure means of achievement, and with special reference to the attainment of your chosen goal, the exercises prescribed in Book Ten of this Course.

SPECIFIC METHODS FOR ACQUIRING FINANCIAL ABILITY

Your Desire must become the background of your mental life, against which all experiences, ideas, emotions and impulses will stand forth in their true colors. It must be the ever-present, ever-watchful sentinel to welcome the friend and to bar the enemy.

There is but one way of bringing this result speedily to pass, and that is by giving up part of your leisure to deliberate and systematic self-training.

And here let us repeat this admonition: You must not make these procedures a mere routine.

To closet yourself with your aspirations at stated hours and to utter certain prayerful formulas is well enough. You will see their beneficial effect from the first day.

But you cannot atone for a sinful week by a sanctimonious Sabbath. You cannot reach your highest mark if you give twenty-three and a half hours of every day to the past and present of your life and only thirty minutes to the future.

You are called upon thoughtfully to determine what things will make for the fullest development of your personality.

You are called upon to so impress these things upon your mind in consciousness as to arouse an absorbing passion for their attainment.

You cannot do this by merely setting part an occasional moment for concentration and prayer. Your purpose, your vision, your faith in the actuality of your vision must be always with you, must saturate your personality.

There is no one to accomplish this for you.

You must help yourself.

And the way to help yourself, the only sure road to fortune, is the way that we have outlined, a way of dream and struggle and self-mastery.

Follow these instructions literally and systematically, and you cannot fail of riches and prosperity.

Specific Applications

THE ULTIMATE AIM

Chapter IV

THE ULTIMATE AIM

HAPPINESS DIVORCED FROM RELIGION

RICHES and Health do not necessarily mean Happiness. If they did, we should find the poor and feeble invariably wretched and the rich and strong always happy.

Look about you. You will observe many who are sleek and luxurious fretting with ennui or proclaiming their miseries in the divorce courts. And that man whose wealth and health are the envy of others may bear a secret burden of griefs and disappointments. On the other hand some of the cheeriest, happiest people you ever knew have been frail of body and meager of purse.

There need be no glamour of sanctity or religious atmosphere about your idea of Happiness.

Happiness is not peculiarly the emolument of religious faith or of any creed.

In more or less transient forms it pays fleeting visits to the most unredeemed of sinners. Napoleon, who "won his way to empire through a sea of blood," and who came at last to unutterable woe, must nevertheless have tasted in his hours of triumph the sweetest forms of Happiness.

Neither is Happiness a definite and invariable condition. It is never the same. What seems Happiness today would be scorned as a base counterfeit tomorrow.

SOURCES OF THE INNER CONTENT

For Happiness runs the complete gamut of pleasurable emotion from the bovine inertia of contentment to the quivering ecstasy of bliss. Happy is the clod who desires nothing, and happy also is the man who is experiencing the fruition of a lifelong desire.

No thoughtful person will contend that Happiness is dependent upon the physical facts of life.

Some are happy in prison; others are wretched in palaces. This man goes to the stake with gladness in his heart; another mounts the steps of a throne and envies the meanest of his subjects.

Indeed, the physical facts of life — that is to say, "things in themselves" — may be said to exert only a very indirect influence, if any, for or against Happiness. Speaking accurately, they do not constitute the environment in which we live.

Sense-impressions are the only assured realities. Our lives are passed in a ceaseless current of sense-impressions.

The sources from which they come may or may not be what our senses report them to be. We cannot know as to that. The mind is a wireless receiving station. No man can know what disturbing influences may intervene between the thing perceived and the mind perceiving it.

So that environment, as an influence, is nothing more nor less than the sum total of sensory images.

Nor is happiness or unhappiness the inevitable result of environment, considered as the sum total of our sensory images, and so as a matter beyond our conscious control. For we may, and do in fact, ignore much the greater part of our sensory images.

Sense-impressions continually throng in upon us from the entire surface of the body. They may convey conflicting messages of one kind or another. Who can tell? No man grasps them all, nor even any considerable part of them.

What we know of the world, what we are conscious of in the world, is not the things-in-themselves that constitute environment, is not even the sum total of our sensory images.

It is those sensory images, and those only, that through the influence of attention as determined by our voluntary and conscious interest are consciously perceived.

POSITIVENESS OF HAPPINESS

What, then, is Happiness? And how is it to be obtained?

Happiness is commonly defined as the pleasurable state of having no unsatisfied desires.

Yet this definition is surely inaccurate. For a desire satisfied is no longer a desire. All living desires are necessarily unsatisfied desires, and this definition amounts to saying that Happiness is the state of desiring nothing.

We cannot deny that this is a form of Happiness.

But it is a poor and unworthy form indeed. It is the lowest possible form. It is a purely negative blessing. It is merely a state of mental inaction. It is the ignoble physical comfort and satisfaction of the sloth and the sluggard.

If this were all that Happiness could offer, it would not justify pursuit.

Happiness, true Happiness, is positive. So far from being the absence of Desire, it finds its very essence in Desire.

True Happiness is the offspring of Desire.

It is more than mere relief from pain; it is more than the security of comfort. It is a positively agreeable condition. It is a definite and conscious delight. It is a vivid and realizing joy. It is a highly emotional state.

True Happiness is founded in Desire. It follows, therefore, that different individuals face different possibilities of happiness according to the range of their desires.

HOW TO REACH THE PINNACLE OF HOPE

He that desires great things will rejoice immeasurably in their pursuit, will revel in their attainment, and even in the event of failure will be consoled by the loftiness of his aspirations. He that desires but little can never reap more than a moderate satisfaction in life, and is without inward resources to sustain him in defeat.

The first rule, then, for the attainment of happiness is this: Aim high.

You need have no fear that your desires may be inordinate. Jesus himself said, "It is your Father's good pleasure to give you the Kingdom."

MAKING LIFE WORTH LIVING

Formulate your desires carefully, thoughtfully, wisely.

Make them the expression of your highest ideals.

Do not hesitate to change them as your views of life broaden with age and experience.

And be assured that such desires as touch the topmost pinnacle of hope are also the expression of your highest mental and spiritual self.

Desire is the basic principle of all evolutionary progress. It is at the bottom of all differentiation of species and all racial development. It is the creative impulse that has caused men to live, to do and to enjoy.

Desire is the ultimate source of all splendid structures, of all colorful pictures, of all heavenly harmonies. It is the source of all beauty, of all personal adornment, of all physical grace and of all mental cultivation. It is the source of all that is good, all that makes life worth the living.

THE CHEAPEST THING IN THE WORLD

Therefore, Desire largely; aim high.

You can never get any more than you desire, and however great your desires, it may come about that every one will be fulfilled.

To desire bravely, to aim high, is one of life's most effective weapons.

And it is the cheapest thing in the world, for it costs absolutely nothing.

Perhaps for this very reason few there are who prize it. Men still insist upon extolling the virtues of poverty and self-effacement, ideas that were first put forward by races whose necks were galled by the yoke of subjection and who found in such philosophies a balm for their pride.

Leave the church of the preacher who tells you that you are but a worm in the dust. Thoughts tend to work their own realization. Say to yourself instead that, as one made in the image of God, you will hold before you such desires as may be worthy of the Almighty.

THE INNER SECRET OF MENTAL HARMONY

Chapter V

THE INNER SECRET OF MENTAL HARMONY

TWO WAYS OF REALIZING DESIRES

AS A man of high aims, it behooves you to realize them, for it is in satisfaction of ambition, realization of desire, that happiness is found.

There are two ways of realizing desire. The first is actual realization; the second is mental realization.

But actual realization without mental realization is of no great consequence as a means to Happiness. There can be no happiness for us in the realization of a desire unless we know about it. The joy comes with the knowledge that what we have so long yearned for has really come to pass.

THE UNFAILING FOUNTAIN OF INWARD JOY

It is the mental picture, with all its associated and exhilarating emotional and energizing elements, that really gives us pleasure.

It is the mental realization, and that only, that brings joy.

Looked at even from the causal standpoint, mental realization holds far the more important place. For no desire can be realized in physical fact that has not first been mentally realized. There can be no creation without antecedent creative thought.

And, finally, the happiness of mental realization is permanent while actual realization is ephemeral.

So that the true, the inner Secret of Happiness is found in this: The Mental Realization of Desire.

Now, the mental realization of a desire need not wait on physical attainment.

More than this, it must not wait on physical attainment.

For every physical achievement is a re-birth. It is the incarnation in the world of matter of that which has had a prior life in the world of mind.

So that to be truly happy one must hold ever in mind his high purpose in life with an unshakable faith in its attainment.

It must be more than the mere portrayal of a hope. It must be more than a mere expectation. It must be conceived in positive faith. It must live today and day by day its coming reality. It must be the picture of the preordained. For by faith, and faith only, can the chasms of life be bridged.

Faith is the foundation stone for all enduring structures — faith in yourself, faith in your object, faith in your ability to compass it.

No one will dispute that desire itself is purely mental. Consciousness is composed in part of sense-perceptions and in part of ideas drawn from sub consciousness. Both have associated with them emotional elements and motor impulses.

Desire is a mental picture composed wholly of thought elements drawn from past experience and associated with agreeable emotional elements. Like all other mental pictures, it has its appropriate and associated motor impulses working toward such muscular activity as will tend to realization.

Ideas have an inherent energy. The more vividly the picture of what we want is painted in consciousness, the more distinct and impressive will all its elements become.

Add a few deft touches to the mental picture. See the thing in the present instead of in the future, done instead of in the doing, won instead of in the winning. The sense of its agreeableness will become more and more pronounced. The impulses to action will strain more and more powerfully in the motor paths. Desire is "growing." It becomes a longing, a yearning, an irresistible demand.

BAD TEMPER, DESPONDENCY, AND FAILURE

This is animate Desire. This is creative thought as distinguished from reverie. This is the kind of mental picture that fills the mind of the "man of vision." This is the kind of thinking that is an unfailing fountain of Happiness. This is Desire conceived in unalterable Faith.

Thoughts are back of all creative impulse.

Whatever there may be of evil or sin, sorrow or suffering or sickness in all the world, it has its origin in thought.

The old idea that a man's bad temper comes from his dyspepsia has given way to the knowledge that his dyspepsia more probably comes from his bad temper. The old idea that a man's despair is due to his failure yields to the knowledge that his failure is more likely due to his despair.

Evil, hopeless thoughts are the cause of all the misery in the world. Aspiring and creative thoughts are the real fairy godmothers of life. They wave the magic wand of an intense desire, a Desire inspired with Faith, and health and riches and happiness shower upon us.

What is the mental machinery by which Thought, Desire, Faith and Happiness may be controlled?

We have seen that the entire content of consciousness, sense-perceptions and memories, is the handiwork of attention.

HOW TO CONTROL THE INNER ATTITUDE

But interest fixes the attention and determines just how its selective work shall be performed. And interest itself is but the creature of habit, the reflection of the mental pictures that are habitually dwelt upon.

Attention selects from the current of sensory images those elements only that fit into the habitual stage-setting of the mind. All others pass unperceived into subconscious oblivion.

Let three men look upon some great and portentous spectacle like the San Francisco fire. The emotional attitude of each, whether of awe, curiosity, hope, despair or pity, depends upon the elements he unconsciously selects as appropriate to his habitual mental setting.

The control of the emotional attitudes, then, is wholly a matter of attention.

You are a free agent. You are the master of your own mental ship. You can steer it where you will. You can think such thoughts, and such thoughts only, as are agreeable to you. You can at any moment produce in consciousness the living image of those things that you desire.

And though the image fades as quickly as it came, it has brought you a momentary happiness.

Obviously, all that is required to make your Happiness lasting is continuous right-thinking, the habit of mentally realizing your desires.

HOW TO ACQUIRE POISE, SERENITY, PEACE

Chapter VI

HOW TO ACQUIRE POISE, SERENITY, PEACE

HOW TO DISPEL SADNESS, GLOOM, REMORSE

YOU can make or mar the Happiness of every moment. For you have within you at every moment the power to thrust before the eye of consciousness a joyous picture of attainment.

Therefore, if the past holds memories that carry with them sadness and remorse, refuse to think of them for a single instant. Drive out of your mind all memories that hold the sting of an irretrievable failure. Drive out all pictured doubts and fears and gloomy forebodings.

Quit making plans and specifications for the mausoleum in which to bury your dead hopes. Bury them now.

Run from the contaminating voice of the prophet of evil. He is the corrupter of thought. Shun the dismal croaker of defeat. He is the assassin of Victory.

There is but one way to do this. It is useless to try to avoid tasting over again the bitter fruits of the past unless your mind is fed with other foods.

Therefore, fill it completely with other thoughts, with creative thoughts, with happy thoughts. Leave no chamber in your mental dwelling untenanted, for if you do it will be haunted with the dreadful phantom of a former tragedy or the grisly specter of some passion that may drain your resources in wasteful physical excess.

Heaven and Hell are within you. Your joy, your peace, your grief and your despair — you carry them all about with you every moment of the day and night.

Just as every sensory experience you ever had was in some faint degree pleasant or distasteful, so every thought in sub consciousness has its emotional element of happiness or gloom.

Think creative thoughts with the intensest faith, and your path in life will be spread with the flowers of a perennial light-heartedness.

THE SINGLE HIGHWAY TO SELF-FULFILMENT

To one who has carefully followed us through all the lessons that have gone before it is needless to point out that what we are here urging upon you as the means to Happiness is nothing more nor less than Concentration — concentration in this case that will inhibit all conflicting emotions and will focus your attention upon the triumphant attainment of the thing you covet.

Turn back with us for a moment. Behold, the three paths, to Success, to Health, to Happiness, have all converged into a single broad and level highway.

In each case the conclusion was arrived at along different lines of reasoning. But you will agree that the arguments have all been consistent in logic and based upon assumptions justified by the discoveries of modern mental science.

It seems most remarkable that in every case our researches have brought us to the same door.

It is even more remarkable that our analysis of what constitutes real happiness and our analysis of the mental processes involved have brought us to know that as to Success and Happiness not only the same kind of process, but the identical procedure, is indicated.

In the pursuit of Health through Concentration, we found it necessary to concentrate the mind upon the bodily operation which it was desired to stimulate. In seeking Success and Happiness, we have learned that the same procedure is necessary — to formulate a purpose, a living desire, and then to concentrate our mental energies upon its achievement.

Here is striking evidence of the fact so often preached, that the highest happiness lies in the faithful pursuit of a beloved ideal.

Clearly, Success and Happiness go hand in hand, but always with the qualification emphasized in the fore part of this volume. It must be success without a sting. It must be success rightfully acquired. It must be success "without deprivation or loss to others."

For this is the only true Success. All else is a transparent sham, "a fiery crown that turns the brain to ashes."

THE COMPASS OF CONCENTRATION

True Happiness and true Success are flowers from the same stem. As mental concentration unites all one's energies in the concordant working of one's plans, So it yields also the mental harmony that is Happiness.

Direct your Thinking, and you are master of your fate. Steer your ship by the Compass of Concentration, and all the seas of life will tranquilly reflect the blue of the unclouded sky. Every breeze that blows will fill your sails and speed you toward your haven.

Make immediate use of the knowledge you have gained. Acquire the habit of Concentration — it is a priceless possession. It is the talisman that will bring you Health and Riches, Success and Happiness and Peace.